SEO

The definitive guide to keyword research

Table of content

Introduction-

I want to thank you and congratulate you for downloading the book, "*SEO: The definitive guide to keyword research* ".

This book contains proven steps and strategies on how to create the best strategies to improve your site rankings and also learn SEO like a pro and to the how to make the ultimate keyword research for your business.

People who are involved in SEO at any level should consider this book invaluable. This includes web developers, development managers, marketing people, and key business people. If SEO is not your profession, then this book may serve perfectly. However, if you are or want to become an SEO practitioner, you will likely want to read it from cover to cover.

You probably are the proud owner of an online business, be that an informational website or a niche site that affiliates to courses or any other type of products. Even though, one thing is for sure: web traffic it's important and comes from many sources such as direct traffic on your website, social media platforms or paid advertising. To ensure that your website it's receiving traffic like crazy and also converts visitors into clients continue reading and you will be amazed.

Thanks again for downloading this book. It will represent the best source that you need for learning SEO and keyword research to the ultimate level. I hope you enjoy it!

Chapter 1: Keyword Research That Works

In SEO world it's a big talk about content and social triggers and so on. It's easy to get lost in details and to forget about what is suppose to be the foundation and also the most important part of SEO and that being: **keyword research.**

I will be as direct as possible with you, keyword research it's almost everything when it comes to SEO, you can't talk about SEO without keywords, there it's no such thing without them.

A quote from a well-known internet marketer that I think it's proper to describe the importance of keyword research it is the fallowing: "Keywords are like a compass for your SEO campaigns: they tell you where to go, whether or not you're making progress. "

Why is it so important to understand how to do a proper keyword research?

This will reveal you what your market desires are, what you can aspect from the market how "hot" or how "cold" it is the market that you are going into or even more important if it is a market and if worth creating a product for that market.

For a better understanding of what keyword research really is, I will say that represents how market research it's made in 21 century and how marketing it's being changed.

GETTING PRACTICAL: To take advantage of keywords let's learn how to find them and also how to use them

Doing a proper keyword research it's the most important part of proper SEO as I said earlier, mastering the art of keyword research will benefit you more by the fact that you will understand your customer better than your competition.

How keyword selection usually looks like:

1. Find some keywords that your customers might look for(not even something relevant sometimes)
2. Try some of the keywords in the Google Keyword Planner tool, or "Galaxy" or any other keyword research tool that it's available on the market and receive some data.
3. Usually, pick the seed keyword that has the most competition and it's the less profitable or relevant for that part of research.

But with the right keywords I can promise you that everything it's going to change because having the right keyword will help you a lot when you are tailoring the "on-page SEO" and will skyrocket your website to the top searches on Google instantly, giving you more traffic, more leading and eventually in the final phase more sales.

I . FIRST STEP

The first step before going for keyword research tool it's to identify the niche topics in the industry that you are going. Once you identified the niche topics you are good to go to find the keywords that we have been talking about.

Niche Topics: Well let's try for example the word "baseball", some things related to baseball will pop into your head like ball, stadium, players, rules, game. But when you enter the word "baseball" into Google Keyword Planner maybe other keywords will appear and may not be related to what you were thinking, to put it in another way Google Keyword Planner it's giving you the most appropriate results for your keyword.

mlb	1 K – 10 K
baseball games	100 – 1 K
baseball scores	10 – 100
mlb live	10 – 100
mlb scoreboard	10 – 100
mlb teams	10 – 100
baseball standings	10 – 100
mlb baseball	10 – 100
espn baseball scores	10 – 100

So that's a very important thing because as soon as you see this you will understand that some keywords are almost impossible to rank for because all people are ranking for the same keywords as you are so that's why we have to get back to identify niche topics.

A niche topic we can define it as a topic that your target will consume it, your customer will consume it to be precise or it's interested in that subject. To put it more simple it's not a specific keyword it's a broad topic.

While your research may show you some great keywords you must have in mind that are dozens and dozens out there the catch it's in the fact that are really hard to find so basically that's the whole deal. That's why the niche topics are the easiest way to get relevant keywords that may be untapped by others till now.

Customers are interested in a couple of niches, in a couple of subjects related, they care about that, for example, somebody interested in baseball may search for:

- How to play baseball
- Baseball caps
- Baseball jacket
- How to strike like a pro in baseball
- How to run faster

Now I guess you are getting an understanding of how things work, even though the seed keyword may be baseball, the big niche baseball your customer or customers can be interested in many other niches that can be unique.

"How to run faster" can be easily the topic of an article on the topic: "run faster like a baseball pro" niche markets are usually small, they are not too large. Also, the same thing I can say about "baseball jacket" or "baseball caps".

Niche markets can bring you up to 10 more profitable keywords with low search volume and added together will create a low competition keyword list that will help you a lot.

Create a niche topic list

Come up with at least 5 different Niche markets, think about something that is relevant and good enough to find keywords. For baseball out of my head, I came with the fallowing:

- How to strike better
- Nutrition for athletes
- Improve resistance
- Baseball shoes
- Vitamins for athletes

It helped me a lot to create a profile for the eventual customer so I had in consideration the fallowing:

- Gender
- Income generated
- Age
- Hobbies that may have
- Goals and what wants to accomplish

Depending on your niche you have different profiles for your customers so its better to get an idea about your client, Michel, 41 years old, makes 70,000$ per year, he is spending time with his son playing baseball and his goal for his son is to play in a big team.

Forums are another great way to find where your target audience may be all you have to do it's to make a search like this: "keyword" + "forums" and check the results.

Wikipedia Table of contents

Here is a recourse that I consider to be a goldmine of niche research and I must admit that I haven't been using it as much as I should. Well, Wikipedia it's a well know website, an online encyclopedia where you can find the best information's written by experts in industry and also lots and lots of topics to research on.

My suggestion for you is to make the search on Wikipedia on your subject, in this case being baseball and enter in your broad niche. You will receive a lot of information's on your subject, till now nothing new, everything it's clear. Wikipedia will structure the result as "Contents" and there you will have a lot of information to investigate on and see what is relevant for you or what it's not relevant in that situation for you. You also will have related results for your search or information's related to the "Main article". Clicking on secondary articles will give even deeper and valuable information's and "sub-niches" that can have valuable keywords, all you have to do at that point is to verify them, to see the score of that keyword.

Contents [hide]

Example for another source it's Reddit, make a search to find what results you will have and you will be surprised what you can find and how valuable it's the information offered. Consider searching on Reddit as "homework" for today. Find topics, find an audience and take notes.

At this moment you should have identified a large group of niche topics and we should be able to find some keywords finally.

When I started learning about SEO I found the following concept, very used by marketers, they divide keywords into three main categories: head, body and of course long tail. Single word keywords usually are highly competitive but no conversion, the phrases with 2-3 words are having medium competition and medium conversion and finally, the 4+ word phrases have high conversion and low competition and that its what we are looking for, low competition and high conversion.

Head Keywords: in general are single word keywords that have usually very very big search volume and very big competition, for, example, publishing, muscle, sports and so on. They are very broad include a lot of results that you may not be interested in so my suggestion is to stay away from the single word keywords.

Body keywords: body keywords are 2-3 word phrases and they usually have a normal or decent search volume, my estimation is at least 2,500 searches per month, but the good thing it's that are more specific that head keywords and obviously it's better to find this type of keywords but still not good enough.

Long tail keywords: finally we got the most important keywords, the long tail that are 4+ word phrases they are the most specific out of them, are phrases like "affordable protein powder for students" they have the less search volume and the lowest competition, all put together from the list of keywords that you are aiming for, for sure everything it's clear till now for what we are looking for.

It is very important to include all of them because some of the body keywords hit a good search volume and I have to say that it's a problem with long tail keywords, usually, you get around 100-1000 searches per month for that long tail keywords. In other order of ideas to get a lot of searches from that long tail keywords, you need to put out a lot of articles maybe hundreds of articles and every article needs to be optimized around that long tail keyword.

Chapter 2: How to use Google Keyword Planner

Google Keyword Planner

Some things are not going to change to soon, we need data, without data we can't measure anything we can't take decisions so in order to get that we are going to use a couple of tools, as a marketer or future marketer you need to create a list of tools that serve you and help you in your work. A tool for keyword research it will be for sure something that you are going to need. In this situation, we are going to take a look at Google keyword Planner how it works, how can help us and also how important it is in our research. Till now I hope that everything it's clear, if not, just read again this part of the book and for sure you will understand how simple and also beautiful it's SEO and also internet marketing, so now let's continue.

One of the best tools out there is Google Keyword Planner the tool for Google, and fortunately, the big boss, Google, gave us this free tool. This tool it is primarily designed for advertisers to be used with Google AdWords and nowadays you can't use Google Keyword Planner without having a running campaign on Google AdWords, but still, can take a look.

Step 1: Now let's access Google Keyword Planner, be sure to have a Google AdWords account also and if you don't have you can set a new account in a couple of minutes very easy.

You will need primarily your e-mail address and a website, well your website in this situation. Just by following those steps you will have set up the account instant.

Step 2: Login to your Google AdWords account, go and click on "Tools" its near reports and will give you access to a drop-down menu where you will see "Keyword Planner" and of course click it to enter.

Now that you are in Keyword Planner you will three dedicated SEO tools for searching new keywords using a phrase, for searching volume data and trends and for multiple keyword lists. Let's choose a tool and be careful this is an important part of our research, please have in mind that you will receive results that are very close to the seed keyword.

Find new keywords and get search volume data

▾ Search for new keywords using a phrase, website or category

Enter one or more of the following:
Your product or service

baseball

Your landing page

www.example.com/page

Your product category

Enter or select a product category

Targeting ?

All locations

All languages

Google

Negative keywords

Date range ?

Show avg. monthly searches
for: last 12 months

Customize your search ?

Keyword filters

Keyword options
Show broadly related ideas
Hide keywords in my account
Hide keywords in my plan

Keywords to include

Get ideas

The first option " Search for new keywords using a phrase, website or category ". **Your product or service** it's the place where you enter your seed keyword I recommend 1-3 word keyword, not to get something too broad.

Your landing page it's addressed more to advertisers using AdWords and **Your Product category** you can use it if you want access to Google's database on different industries. For sure I recommend playing around for a little with the tool to get familiar and see how easy is to use is in case it is the first time using Google Keyword Planer. You can customize your search by targeting more by language, a period of search and location.

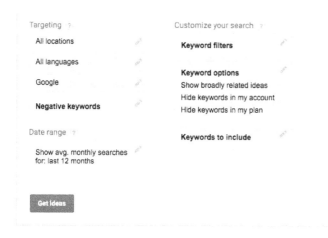

Keyword filters: this is a filter that allows you to filter some of the searches that you make so that means that you can select, you can select even the volume of searches that the keyword can have or the bid that to you how to appear for the keyword.

Get search volume data and trends : second part of keyword planner, this part is more for long list of keywords or if you want to check the volume of searches for those keywords, this is not a tool to generate new keywords but to check the keywords that you already have, you can also add CSV files which can be very useful instead of typing, targeting it's another option that you have and it's included, per say the country that you want to make the search.

Multiply keyword lists to get new keywords: the third part of keyword planner makes groups of keywords and combines them in hundreds of other combinations of keywords, very rarely I use this tool. In most of the cases, I'm interested just in the first one "Search for new keywords using a phrase, website or category". Now that we have everything clear, write the keywords that you are interested in and hit "Get ideas".

Here is how results are looking when you are making a search:

Find keywords   Review plan

Ad group ideas   Keyword ideas

Columns ▾   ⬇ Download   Add all (424)

Keyword (by relevance)	Avg. monthly searches	Competition ↓	Suggested bid	Ad impr. share	Add to plan
baseball cardigans	10 – 100	High	RON12.34	–	
slim fit baseball jacket	10 – 100	High	RON2.36	–	
leatherman jacket	1K – 10K	High	RON4.21	–	
boys baseball jacket	100 – 1K	High	RON3.28	–	
baseball cardigan womens	10 – 100	High	RON1.77	–	
baseball hoodie jacket	10 – 100	High	RON3.85	–	
black and grey baseball jacket	10 – 100	High	RON5.53	–	
red and blue baseball jacket	10 – 100	High	RON0.37	–	
baseball bomber jacket womens	100 – 1K	High	RON4.63	–	
buy baseball jacket	10 – 100	High	RON0.80	–	
mens varsity jacket	1K – 10K	High	RON4.48	–	

Targeting:
All locations
All languages
Google
Negative keywords

Date range
Show avg. monthly searches for: last 12 months

Customize your search
Keyword filters

Keyword options
Show broadly related ideas
Hide keywords in my account
Hide keywords in my plan

Keywords to include

The breakdown for what you are seeing on the page. In the upper left part of the page, you have "Keyword planner" that shows you the targeting for the location, language, the search engine and negative keywords that you have, those are targeting tools that you can use to be as specific as you want in your search. Date range, that can be used to select the period of the search, for example, if you want Google to show you results from last 12 months or more. The last options are for keyword filters, volume search and bid as I said and other keyword options that are offered.

Taking a look at the table we can see "Search terms" there you will find the exact keywords that you typed and you are receiving data. "Keywords" by relevance is the list that you receive for most relevant results from Google with the options that you selected(or not).

Avg. monthly searches as the name sais it's representing the number of searches that are made for that specific keyword during a month period of time, also this can change depending on events that are taking place, let's say searching for "Christmas gifts" when Christmas it's coming in December instead of searching in June.

Competition: it's giving you information's on how much others are investing in advertising for that specific keyword, keeping the things simple on a keyword that has more competition the bid will be bigger and one that may have less competition the bid will be smaller.

Suggested bid: The higher the suggested bid obviously the more traffic it's going to be on that keyword, be careful on bidding on keywords and the campaigns that you are making on Google, you are working with money, real money.

I've continued my search on "baseball jackets" and now we are going to take a look at "Ad group ideas".

Hitting on a group of keywords will give you more keywords so that is a good thing because you are receiving more keywords that you can test and see what it's better to for you let's say Men's baseball, will give me more keywords to look on, and from here I can find even more keywords to test for score, volume, difficulty and so on, the more keywords we have the better. You can sometimes find keywords or niche topics directly from the group ideas as the first result that Google gave me in this search.

Now let's get to "Keyword ideas", we discussed earlier this table and the columns and what every column means but in my opinion there are 3 main categories to keep in mind when choosing your keywords: search volume, commercial intent, organic SEO competition. Looking at Avg. monthly search's you will see that it's not giving you exact data you have results let's say from 100K - 1M so it's not relevant enough, we need clear information. But there is a little trick that we can do without activating an AdWords campaign. Find a keyword from the suggested keyword that you got from Google and you want to use in future to target and click on it and then "add to plan" it will be on the right side of your table. Clicking on add to plan will give you more information's about bid, clicks, and costs. Click on "review plan" and from here you will receive more data, Google will assume that this is an add that you are creating and will make a prediction for that ad on how is going to behave. Look at the number of "impressions" and you can make a clear idea on that keyword and this is how many people search for keywords every day.

Let's say that you got 100 impressions on that keyword all you have to do it's just to multiply with 30 and now you got the volume searches for that month, simple as that. Now all you have to do its do get to work, choose your keywords, follow the steps that I've indicated and taken notes on the results that you receive from Google, see you on next chapter of the book.

Chapter 3: How to Find Long Tail Keywords

All marketers love Google, for the same reason, it's giving you valuable information's about market, but all market also hate it for the same reason, your competition has access to the same information's as you have, and it's a content work and a constant chase for the best keywords, strategies, and tactics and so on, internet it's changing so fast and things are advancing in such a fast way that you can't close you eyes even for a second.

Now let's start looking on "Searches related to", have you seen that when you are looking on Google at the bottom of the page you can see "Searches related to" giving you more alternative searches which represents a very very good source of keywords.

Just make a search on Google and then jump directly to the bottom of the page. I've searched for baseball to see what Google gives me and those are the results at the bottom of the page, which as I said are representing another source of keywords.

baseball **reguli**

baseball **mlb clasament**

baseball **games**

baseball **live**

PRO TIP: I tip that I've got reading an article on a well-known blog about SEO is select one of the keywords that you got on "Searches related to" and go with it in Google's bar and make a search and then go down again to "Searches related to" and see what keywords it's showing you again, this is very important to go as deep as you can with your search, don't get discouraged by the number of results that you have, that's a good thing, take one by one the most relevant keywords for you and try till you find the most relevant results for you search that a very important thing for a good keyword research if you want to succeed or to find the best keywords for your business/website.

As I said at the start of the book when making a search on Google for more keywords go a type "keyword" + "forum" you will be amazed by the results that you will get after this search.

Let's say for example baking + discussions will bring you results from Q & A that are found on internet, on forums, on boards or any other website that is a discussion, when you find forums that are active or seem to be active look at the most discussed topics, search for the hottest subject in this care on a cooking forum the subject may be about bread or cookies. Those are representing extremely good keywords to try in Google Keyword planner or as I said any other keyword research tool in case you want to use something else, data it's our friend. In about 1 minute you can get over 20 new keywords, short tail or long tail keywords, "how much flour to use", "it healthier corn flour than X flour ?" sounds pretty easy? Well it is, the only things that are required are your energy and your time, but don't rush it, you can't make any SEO on your website if you don't target the right audience so be patient.

Another great advice about a tool that's in my arsenal it's the website soovle.com, a free tool for long tail keyword suggestions that you receive from the biggest search engines out there like: Google, Wikipedia, Yahoo and so on.

You will type your keyword and then you will receive a lot of long tail keywords from the websites mentioned. You can download a CSV file with the most searched keywords on those search engines

Another great way to find keywords to conduct your research is to type you seed keyword in Google's search bar and without pressing enter you will receive from Google some long tail keywords that are searched and important. So this is another great "tool" that you have in your arsenal, there are a lot, I mean a lot of keyword research tools or methods to find keywords and also valuable keywords, just choose the methods or tools that you like the most and master them.

Google Webmaster Tools

Sometimes you will see that you may be ranking on Google on pages that you were not even optimizing or looking for to rank, obviously for long tail keywords.

You can find those type of 2nd 3rd-page keywords in Google search console.

Google Trends

This tools from Google(I hope that everybody saw till now that Google offers you a lot, I mean a lot of tools to help you with but go crazy, you won't have to master all of them, it's important just to establish that 20% that will produce the 80%).

I've made a search for "coffee" to see what are the most relevant results that I can get for last 30 days, it looks like it's constant we have some reference here on how "hot" or "cold" is the word and from how It looks it's pretty stable in Google searches.

I've also made a search on "Snapchat" on last 5 years, it looks like it's a big growth for Snapchat in Google searches for good reasons, the application was just exploding in popularity in last years and we can see that clear in Google Trends.

IMPORTANT TIP: Scroll down the page and you will see related queries, this is a very important because you can see recently searched information's about your seed keyword using long tail or short tail keywords.

1 how to snapchat

2 instagram snapchat

3 instagram

4 emoji snapchat

5 delete snapchat

Another tool that I can recommend you is Google Correlate, which is not a well-known tool offered by Google that shows you correlated keywords.

Quara.com it's a Q&A website that I strongly advise you to check, you can search through the questions out there, also post questions to see what are the points of interest and how many people are reacting on the subject that you are researching.

My last tool for you that I present in this chapter of the book it's keyword tool.io a great free tool that I recommend to use. In my opinion one of the greatest tools for generating long tail keywords that are relevant and test. All you have to do it's just enter your seed keyword and the tool will do the rest for you giving lots and lots of long tail keywords.

Keyword Tool

Get 750+ Google Keyword Suggestions For Free

I hope that you enjoyed this chapter on keyword research tools see you on next chapter and keep in mind just choose one or two tools and take action.

Chapter 4: How to Determine a Keyword's Commercial Intent

Looking back at mistakes that I've made in past I can easily find one mistake that a lot of people are doing, including myself and that is not spending enough time on commercial intent. What does that mean? To say it in a simple but not complete way, it's about the money in the market. Are money in the market, are money to be spent in that market or not, a very important thing if you are looking to create a long-term business and a sustainable business. You need cash flow into your business so the commercial intent is something that you really have to take in consideration if exists or not.

So as I said some of the SEO experts out there are considering commercial intent to be more important than the search volume.

I was reading an article about commercial intent from an internet marketer emphasizing how important is be clear about commercial intent, one of his first websites was having around 100.000 unique visitors per month. At first, I was just wondering how much he was making from that website, 10k, 20k, no 40k per month? Well, in reality, we barely were making 500$ from that website. He explained then that when he chose the keywords for the website he focused on search volume and completely ignored commercial intent.

In other almost 100% of his traffic was visiting his website just for informational purposes, not to buy something. So be a little bit more specific and use a radical example, the commercial purpose of a keyword changes completely based on the website or platform that you enter. If you are going on Amazon I can't even talk about commercial intent because you are there with the purpose of buying something, the visitor doesn't need to be converted at all, but if you are writing informational articles including keyword search: that may help you to rank but it's no commercial intent behind then, obviously that you are not going to make any money, in other words, you must have in your mind keywords that monetize in final.

I'll divide keywords after commercial intent into four keyword classes:

1. "Buy" or "Buy now" keywords
2. Product Keywords
3. Informational Keywords
4. Tire Kicker Keywords

1. "Buy" or "Buy now" keywords usually those ones are the keywords that people use before making any kind of purchase. People searching using those type of keywords usually are ready to make the purchase, they know exactly for what are looking to buy.

Just to make an idea below you have a couple of keywords that are used by customers:

- Deal
- Shop
- Buy

- Shipping
- Free
- Discount
- Promotion

To give you an example of how those keywords may be used: Go Daddy promotion, T-Shirts free shipping.

As you may thinking those keywords are very profitable because they convert excellent, look in your research for those type of keywords, search for the competition and how expensive would be to advertise on them if you need.

2. Product Keywords is another category of keywords that people are searching for, they can be brand names, services, products. People that are searching using product keywords don't have the same intent to make a purchase like people using "buy now" keywords, a little bit harder to convert but not impossible, but at the end of the day, they still convert pretty well.

Product Keywords may look something like this:

- Review
- Preview
- Unboxing

- Nike
- Apple
- Coaching program
- MacBook Pro (specific product search)
- Affordable
- Quality

Combinations of keywords that you may aspect can be MacBook Pro review, or Quality shoes and so on. Not the same intent to make the purchase but still, they convert well.

3. Informational Keywords, searching on the internet, you will see that the majority of the keywords are informational, even looking for a book, article, recipe it's an informational keyword search. Talking about people making a search using this type of keywords they don't have the intent to buy something, they are looking more to information's, to look for opinions, to ask questions and to find out more about what the topic that is searching for.

Informational keywords look something like:

1. How to: how to cook, how to repair something, how to make something

2. Best way to best ways to do lose weight, best ways to make money
3. Ways to: ways to get healthier, ways to run faster
4. I need to: I need to book a room, I need to resolve x problem

5. The Tire Kicker Keywords they are not a type of keywords that I would recommend to convert, they don't represent in my opinion a point of interest when you are doing SEO and I'll give you a couple of examples to get a better understanding:

- Free
- Torrent
- Download

Those type of keywords usually are not used when you are trying to make an acquisition, you want information and you want it now and fast not a product or service. The only thing that may happen is the person that is looking for a torrent may visit your website and click on ads.

General information's about Commercial Intent

The four category of keywords is reflecting the intent of the customer to buy something or not. At the end, I don't consider anything worst than ranking #1 for your keyword and not being able to make a sale. So let's talk a little bit about quick techniques that you can use you get objective information on how valuable is your traffic that is coming on your website.

1.AdWords Suggested Bid

AdWords Suggested Bid is known also as "Average CPC" by the most people is one of the ways that you can use to test and see the commercial intent of a keyword. If you know how much is paying an advertised per keyword that can be really valuable information for you, paying 1$ or 10$ per click can be a really valuable information.

How to do it:

Login into AdWords and go to Keyword Planner tools and make a search using "Search for new keywords using a phrase, website or category" the suggested bit category will appear in the table you made the search.

Looking at the differences of prices you can create an opinion on how competitive are the keywords and the commercial intent.

AdWords Competition is a very useful information that you receive about "Low", "High","Medium" are representing metrics even though it's not the most precise information that you get it's still useful to get a better understanding. Also, another way to check AdWords competition is by searching your keyword on Google and check how many ads are created for that keyword.

If you are looking at a ton of ads than you know for sure that you are looking at a very competitive keyword and also the conversion it's very good for that one, that is also explaining the price for suggested bid in Google keyword planner. But with all that data it's not clear enough how competitive is the keyword or how worthy is to take it into consideration. See you in next chapter to discuss even more about that!

Chapter 5: How to make a keyword Competition Analysis

Now we got to the point we how about how to search for keywords, we have an idea about tools that we can use in our search, what to test, sources where you can find keywords, also about how to use Google Keyword Planner, type of keywords about their structure and also now after getting all those information's how to check for their commercial intent. Let's talk more about how to make a keyword competition analysis.

We have some popular keywords at this moment and also we checked for their intent, so that's a very good thing BUT we still don't know if they really are worthy or not, my suggestion at this moment is to go on Google and to check out the competition on Google's first page of results, so let's do that.

First thing will be that when you are making the search and receive on first page just big brands, authoritative brands, that will not be a good thing, too hard to compete with names well known and also with budgets for advertising so it would be a good idea to look at the next keyword on your list of keywords.

Another good thing it's that a keyword competition analysis it's a great way to evaluate competition on general, a great opportunity to find keywords with good search volume and also maybe find new keywords or better keyword with little competition or no competition.

What that all means? Well, keywords with great search volume and little to no competition will mean for you less content to post on your website, also fewer links and savings in your budget when promoting to get your spot on the first page of searches on Google.

In this chapter will talk more about how to quickly evaluate keywords competition in Google for organic searches results.

We are going to use "The MozBar" for this part of the book. "The Moz Bar" is a free tool for your browser that you can install by going on the website moz.com and take a look at their product category. After downloading the tool just go and install and activate it.

When you do a search using MozBar you should see information from Mozbar displayed like that:

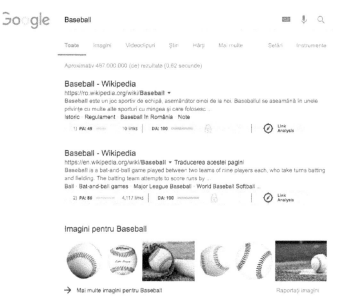

Let's talk about Page-Level Authority. It's an old "myth" about Google that it ranks pages, not sites.

Even the though a site's presence, an authority it's something very important, one of the #1 factors in a page's ability to rank in Google is the authority of that page so it looks like that myth it's pretty true.

A good way to make a measurement of a page's authority is using Moz's Page Authority. Make a search on

Google after you activate the Moz bar and you will see in the PA section the number of results. Don't panic its ok for a SERP to have a couple of high PA results on the first page that the case for the majority of high or medium keywords in searches out there. My recommendation is to also look for low PA and to take in consideration to give a chance also to those keywords.

Domain authority and Brand presence

Well, I'm pretty sure that you know that Google appreciates a lot of big brands, big names and when I'm saying that I'm talking about Wikipedia, I'm talking about Facebook, about CNN and the list goes on.

Those ones are representing without any doubts Authority websites and have a hard presence of in Google searches. How do you translate that? Well, it is quite simple when you evaluate a keyword completion you also want to take a small look at sites Topics: are competing with NOT just pages that you see. In general, I can say that results with HIGH PA or HIGH DA are super competitive. In this situation, you need to see on first results data with low PA and low DA. Those ones are representing keywords that are really easy to rank for. This is a very important lesson, the website authority matters more than you think, take that into consideration! Amazon, ESPN, YouTube will be some names that you will encounter in your search.

Link Profile

In case you have been learning or doing SEO for a long period of time that you will understand better what we are talking about, experience in this game in special with metrics it's something that can be very misleading. If you are looking at a keyword that looks competitive but you are not sure about that, there might have as well some black hat SEO behind what are you seeing in those top 10 positions on Google, for those that don't know black hat SEO is representing a form of SEO that is very risky and it's not ok to be applied and Google could take down your website, in my opinion it doesn't worth to even mess with Grey hat, not even talking about Blackhat SEO.

 Getting back to what we were discussing it will be very hard for you to rank a keyword in the situation of a very aggressive competition.

       Take an URL and paste it in Ahrefs and then go on Backlinks sections, you will see the top 10-20 links and their link profile. Being there will be very easy for you to determine if that page uses black hat SEO.

 Links coming from these places have the tendency to indicate a black hat link profile because:

- Article directories
- Blog networks
- Low-quality web directories

Also, I suggest you keep an eye on well optimize anchor texts.

On-Page SEO. You might know that on-page SEO can make the same type of difference like keyword research, something fundamental. I strongly recommend you to pay attention to on-page SEO for your first competitors and when I say, competitors, I'm talking about first page results on Google. The first results are representing the titles of the articles that you see displayed there. Usually, have appropriate keywords, they don't differ too much and also the heading used might be H1 or H2, in that case, we can talk about a well-optimized page.

Content Quality

We talk about keywords, we talk about domains, tools and so on but not to forget about the content, that may be the number one reason that you get a visitor on your website, having all those requirements met but not having good quality content will not be something that your visitor or future client appreciate.

To put it in another way let's say that you rank for a competitive keyword you will have to compete with the first 10-20 results for that keyword, and if everybody ranks for quality content (which is something that Google appreciates a lot) you will have you stand out, to make yourself visible.

How to check competition for your keyword? Very simple just type it and see the first results that are appearing on Google, it will represent the best source of information that you can get.

If you are writing content by yourself or hiring a ghostwriter for you to write it will help you a lot to take a decision, you may not be able to write about that subject or your level of expertise might not be good enough on that subject, people demand a lot nowadays in term of content and more than that content quality.

Your content must be A+ and should be considered by your visitors the best source of information on that subject.

Another important fact is the length of the article. Here is a very important thing, Google sees the length of your article as what makes an article valuable, so having that in mind we must think about the number of the words that the article has. To keep it simple longer is better. If you are wondering how many words to have your article? 100 words? 200 words? 1000 words? Well, the answer is more content usually over 1000 words but please keep in mind that more content doesn't mean better content. In Google Webmaster Academy course you can learn about creating valuable content answering to all of your questions about quality content and how to deliver value to the person that is reading your article or articles.

Main points must be:

- Useful and informative
- Credible
- High quality
- Engaging
- More useful than content from your competition

Chapter 6: What tools to use for keyword research

We have been talking about keyword research tools and will still continue to talk about this subject. If you consider yourself a serious internet marketer then you have to know about the most important tools for SEO.

Google Keyword Planner will be for sure an important tool that I'll recommend but on the market are tons and tons of other tools offering important features and help in your SEO work. So let's dive deeper into this chapter.

Due to the fact that keyword research is something that can be done very fast you will get experience and be able to find low-competition keywords in a couple of minutes, faster than you will thank. The question is what is the best tool to acquire this skill? Which keyword tool it's the most proper for you or for your business. Will go straightforward about this subject with most important tools that I've been using and I recommend to use and hope that you will find your tool that will help you also in your research. So the top for the most important tools is the following:

1. Moz Keyword Explorer

Moz keyword Explorer it's a new keyword research tool released by the guys from moz.com(if you still don't know them I strongly suggest to check their site and take a look at their articles about SEO) with a lot of exclusive useful features. Do those features make Moz Keyword Explorer a strong competitor for Google Keyword Planner or SEM Rush or any other keyword research tool? Well let's see:

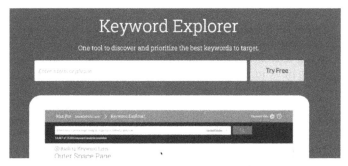

First of all, this is a free tool, so you can have access to their tool without paying or using any trial version, quick and easy. Just type the keyword that you are looking for, short tail or long tail keyword and hit Try Free. I have to mention that you have 2 searches and then you will have to buy Moz Pro but till then its completely free.

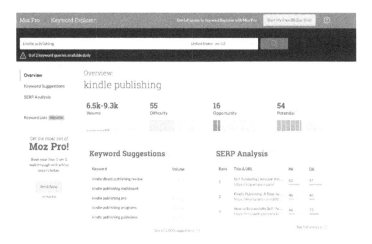

So this is how it looks like, you will receive information's about the volume of the keyword, in this search you can see that I've searched for "kindle publishing" with 6.5k-9.3k volume, with difficulty of 55, the opportunity being 16 and potential 54. It's pretty simple to check how valuable is that keyword or not. Also a little bit lower you have some keyword suggestions in my case are kindle direct publishing review, kindle publishing dashboard, kindle publishing pro and so on, and also a SERP Analysis.

Conclusion: Moz keyword tool is a very simple keyword tool that can be used by beginners and also by advanced SEO guys. It's a solid tool that I strongly recommend you to try if you haven't tried yet.

2. SEM Rush

SEM Rush is the second keyword tool that we are going talk about in this chapter. This tool works a little bit different than other keyword tools that you have tried. In SEM Rush when you are entering your seed keyword you will receive data but that data will be about that keyword that your competition is ranking for already and also of a list of informational keyword to rank for. It's a very useful tool because seeing what keyword is your competition using will be something very useful to check if those keywords are competitive, are profitable, if they are betting on the good keyword or bad keywords.

SEMrush Competitive Data
for Digital Marketing Professionals

We are going to focus on keyword overview analysis for now. Also just testing purposes we are going to use the long tail keyword "kindle publishing" and analyze the results.

You are going to see information's about Volume of the keyword, in this case, being 5,4k and the number of results being 27.4M in the organic search section. In the paid search you will see CPC information's being 53.61 and competition 0.13. Also live updates with CPC Distribution, the Trend, and in the lower part of the page Information about Phrase match keyword and related keywords.

Conclusion: In conclusion, SEM Rush is a very good tool, I would recommend this tool more for advanced SEO people with a little bit more experience in PPC and know how to use keywords for paid campaigns also. SEM Rush, it's for sure a must have in your arsenal, I suggest to go and test this tool, to "play" with it just a couple of moments to see how it works and if you enjoy it.

3. Ahrefs keywords Explorer

Ahrefs keywords Explorer it's one of my favorite keyword research tools, I enjoy a lot using this tool for how complete are the importations that it's giving you, the graphics that are used when the information's are being displayed and also for how easy is to use it, it's simple a very good tool, a clever tool. It has a trial version for two weeks, so you will have enough time to test it and check all the features that the tool has.

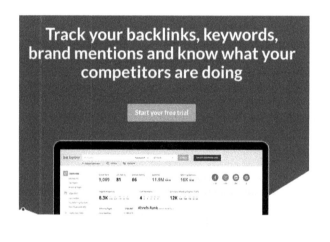

Keywords Explorer

Get thousands of relevant keyword ideas with accurate search volume, keyword difficulty score and advanced metrics like Clicks, Return rate and Parent topic.

kindle publishing

For testing purposes I've taken also "kindle publishing" and know let's take a look at the results that we got out of this research:

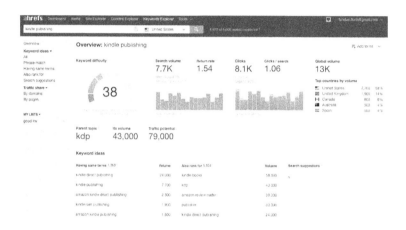

Most important data that I take in consideration are usually from this panel. Ahrefs it's giving you information's about keyword difficulty, in this case being 38, it's giving you information's about search volume, 7.7k, clicks, Global volume, also the parent topic, Kdp. The total volume as we can see it's 43.000 and the potential traffic that the keyword can generate it's about 79.000.

A little bit lower you have information's about a Keyword ideas, that being a long tail keyword, kindle direct publishing, amazon kindle direct publishing and their volume.

Conclusion: Out of those 3 tools this one is my favorite for how simple it is to use it, for me, it's a perfect choice and makes keyword research simple fast and easy. It's not coming with something new, it's not coming with a lot of features but it's designed as a tool that I would recommend to a beginner but also to an advanced SEO person.

The last and final chapter of the book, turning keywords into SEO Content. Finally, the reason of the research to turn those keywords into content for your website. The only role of a keyword analyze it's to finally turn them into content for your website, content it's very important in ranking on Google, don't forget people search by keyword, they watch for the keyword they think in keywords so let's give them what they want.

Now that we have worked hard for searching the keywords, with low-competition, with big search volume, with CPC and high returns it's time to make phrases and turn them into articles. It's important to keep in mind that this content it's meant to rank high in Google searches and will have guidelines to follow while developing content for your website.

Use your title tags as much as possible!

Most people approach the title tag in the following way, in special optimization:

1. They find a keyword for that web page
2. After that, they go and add that keyword to the title tag

3. Finally, they hope that keyword it's going to work and make some miracles

Let's consider that your page title tag it's the most important on-page SEO ranking ingredient(I do consider page title tag as being the most important element) so knowing that let's try to squeeze the most value out of it.

Let's tap into some optimizing techniques, for some short tail and also long tail keywords. Trying to rank for long tail keywords will help you rank quicker because usually it's less competitive and you will see that over time you will be able to rank faster for short tail titles that you have.

For example, you want to rank for "Marketing tips", let's say you found that this keyword has a good search volume and also buyer intent. My advice for you would be: instead of using the title "Marketing tips" you can use a long tail version like this one "Marketing tips: 20 Methods to learn how to market". In this way, you will be able to rank a little bit faster.

Publish Longer Articles

I talked a little bit about the length of the articles a little bit earlier, but I have to say it again: publish longer articles. 1000+, 1500+ word articles will crush a 400-word article on the same subject.

The only downside that I can see in this situation it's the fact that you have to word a little bit more, bigger articles require more research, more work or more money in case you are outsourcing your content.

Your competition might now be that interested to get longer articles and on a long run this will be your advantage, this is a marathon, not a sprint.

Why publishing longer articles with more content it's important?

Well excepting the fact that we are in the era of content where everybody wants to consume content, image, video, audio and of course written content, excepting this part more content means higher rankings in Google. Google loves long articles, considers then as being quality. A research showed that articles with more than 1500 words will help you to rank in the first results easier than shorter articles.

It important because:

- Longer content gives Google more information's about your topic, your main interest on your website and this helps your page to become more relevant.
- A longer article it's important because it's pretty hard to communicate something meaningful to your viewer in 400 words, and this will keep your visitors engaged.
- A longer article will help for your experience on a page for the person that is visiting your blog.
- A longer article will help you with your keyword density

I'm pretty sure that now makes a little bit more sense why longer articles will help you rank better. Test it, try out with 300-word articles, 500-word articles, and 1000 word articles to see what's the result.

Keyword Prominence

Keyword Prominence it related to where your keyword appears on a page, basically, the higher on the page is your keyword the better, Google will appreciate even more your page in that situation.

Make people stay on your website! Google appreciates having visitors that spent a lot of time on your website, this factor it's dependent on UX, you can use the fallowing strategies to make the experience more pleasant for people visiting your website:

- Make first sentences of your articles a little bit shorter. The idea's simple to give people good, quality information's, easy to understand at the start of the article till you hook them.
- Create an experience. You will have to create an experience for the person visiting your website, infographics, videos, quality pictures, good looking fonts and the list can go on and on.
- Use h tag subheadings. If you are publishing long articles I suggest you to use subheaders to split a little bit more your content.

Conclusion

Thank you again for downloading this book!

I hope this book was able to help you to understand how to do a proper keyword research and how keyword research affects SEO and also enjoyed the book!

The next step is to be sure that you fully understand the information, also apply it and read it as frequently as necessary.

Finally, if you enjoyed this book, then I'd like to ask you for a favour, would you be kind enough to leave a review for this book on Amazon? It'd be greatly appreciated!

If you enjoyed the the this book check out other releases that you might like:

Data Analytics: Essentials to master Data Analytics and get your business to the next level

Passive Income: 3 Proven Business Models That Generate Online Revenue to Achieve Financial Freedom